IMAGES ON STONE

THE PREHISTORIC ROCK ART OF THE COLORADO PLATEAU

by Donald E. Weaver, Jr.

W9-BQJ-325

SASKATOON PUBLIC LIBRARY

33/14
31/13
26/06

The Museum of Northern Arizona

Petroglyphs at Red Tank Draw, Arizona. Photograph by Gene Balzer

INTRODUCTION

The sharp noise of rock pounding on rock rose above a subtle background sound of cascading water. It was accompanied by a low chant, echoing softly through the narrow canyon, that originated from a small group of buckskin-attired men sitting in a semicircle. Each man was equipped with well-used hunting implements, a bow and stone-tipped arrows in an animal skin case, a stone knife with a bone or wooden handle, and a tool kit in a small skin pouch. The attention of the small group was focused on one man crouching next to the canyon wall. The man patiently worked at creating a hunting scene on a smooth section of the cliff face. Using a sharpened, fist-sized stone, he had already finished the pecking of a deer and was rapidly completing a standing archer with bow fully drawn. The barbed arrow pointed directly at the body of the deer. The chanting faded into respectful silence as the leader of the group completed the rock drawing. Then, the crouching man rose, spoke a few phrases, and quietly led the group up a steep trail through the canyon cliff and into the surrounding pine forest.

Weak rays of winter sunlight gradually warmed the walls of the rock shelter. Drops of water fell from tree branches encased in glistening ice. Occasionally, a boulder crashed to the canyon floor—breaking the snowy silence. A solitary hunched figure, immobile, faced the back of the overhang. The man, wrapped in a fur blanket, stared at a huge painting of a white, black, and red serpent that was vividly illuminated by the early morning sun. Carefully placed around the man were eagle and hawk feathers, carved pieces of deer antler, rocks and pebbles of unusual shapes, several small skin pouches, and a small black-on-white decorated jar. The shadow of the rock overhang gradually moved downward over the serpent as the sun rose in the sky. By the time the sun reached its highest point, the overhang was completely in shadow. Still, the contemplative figure did not move. In early afternoon, the man began to stir—uttering precise phrases obviously directed to another unseen presence. Periodically, he sang a soft, repetitious chant. Finally, at mid-afternoon, the man again became silent, rose from his sitting position, and began mixing white, black, and red powder that he removed from the animal skin pounches with a thick, syrupy liquid from the jar. He applied the white, black, and red colors over areas of the serpent that had faded, restoring the colors to fresh vividness. When satisfied with his work, he walked along the ledge to a spot where numerous red lines had been painted on the back of the overhang. Carefully, he added one more line to an already lengthy row, turned, and gathered up his possessions. Quickly, as if to get away from something very powerful (and, perhaps, dangerous), the man descended the steep slope below the overhang and walked silently through the snow towards the mouth of the canyon. He turned north at the canyon mouth—moving quickly toward the faint smoke plume rising from a pueblo built against a red cliff.

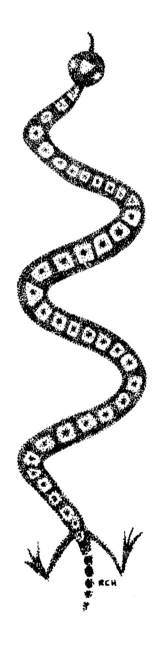

A line of silent masked figures, led by an old man carrying a large sack, walked across the windswept mesa. The group stopped on a barren point overlooking the valley below. There, the masked figures formed two parallel lines facing each other. The old man, chanting softly, opened his sack and slowly sprinkled a handful of corn meal on a large boulder adorned with three petroglyphs—a dancing human-like figure, a serpent, and a spiral. Turning away from the boulder, he walked slowly behind each line and sprinkled corn meal on each of the twenty masked figures. Moving to the very edge of the precipice, he cast a small handful of corn meal in each of the cardinal directions, hesitating longest while facing the jagged peaks visible on the western horizon. Turning, he slowly led the masked figures back to the large pueblo situated on the highest elevation of the mesa. The beat of drums mingled with the sound of shuffling feet and rhythmic chanting throughout the long, hot summer day. By late afternoon, huge, black cumulus clouds were rolling over the mesa. Periodically, flashes of lightning, followed by grumbling thunder, indicated an approaching summer thunderstorm. As the wind rose in velocity, large raindrops began to fall.

Archaeologists believe that the scenes described above are typical of some of the circumstances in which the prehistoric rock art of the Colorado Plateau was produced and used. Rock art was an integral part of functioning dynamic cultures, and as such, it reflected the ebb and flow of prehistory.

Although some writers of pseudo-science would have us believe that the rock art of the New World was produced by space travelers; members of the Lost Tribes of Israel; or wayward Egyptians, Celts, or Phoenicians, scholars believe that is was produced by Native Americans. In fact, the Colorado Plateau, because of the well-documented continuity between prehistoric, historic, and extant Native American groups, provides some of the best evidence in support of this general scientific conclusion.

Many Native American groups that still inhabit portions of the Colorado Plateau have elaborate oral traditions about rock art. The Hopi, for example, associate many petroglyphs with a time called the "gathering of the clans." Clans trace their ancestors back to specific sites with associated rock art—such as the Homolovis, Crack-in-Rock pueblo, Betatakin, and others.

There is no other evidence that supports a Native American origin for rock art. On the Colorado Plateau, rock art designs virtually identical to designs on the local prehistoric pottery are commonplace. Similarly, kivas (subterranean religious rooms) found at Native American prehistoric sites such as Awatovi and Lowry have elaborately painted murals that bear striking resemblances to nearby rock art sites, both in terms of overall composition and individual designs. At Mesa Verde National Park, several of the large cliff dwellings have wall stones with pecked and incised designs very similar to designs at nearby rock art sites.

Although there is abundant evidence, then, to support the conclusion that most, if not all, rock art was produced by prehistoric and historic Native Americans, there is literally no scientific evidence to indicate that other non-Native American groups were responsible. For these reasons, we can say with certainty that the rock art of the Colorado Plateau was produced by the prehistoric hunters, gatherers, and farmers known to us through numerous archaeological investigations and the Native American groups descended from those early people.

PETROGLYPHS AND PICTOGRAPHS
TECHNIQUES AND FUNCTIONS

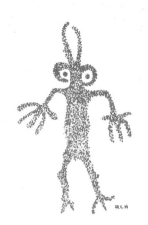

Rock art, a modern misnomer that originated in Europe, is a categorical term that includes purposeful human modification of in-place rock surfaces by pecking, scratching, incising, engraving, drilling, carving, grinding, and painting to produce preconceived images. Thus, the bedrock grinding surfaces that result from grinding activities to produce seed flour are not considered rock art. Decorated pebbles also fall outside the accepted definition of rock art.

Within the broad category of rock art are two generally accepted subcategories. Petroglyphs are images created on rock surfaces by removing, usually by pecking, a portion of the rock surface. Pictographs are images created on rock surfaces by applying pigments, usually as paints. Of course, combinations of the two do occur occasionally.

Although rock art occurs throughout the United States (including Alaska and Hawaii), the greatest known concentrations occur in California, the Great Basin (Nevada and western Utah), the Columbia Plateau (Washington, Oregon, and Idaho), and the Southwest (New Mexico, Arizona, eastern Utah, southwestern Colorado, and western Texas). Certainly, the Colorado Plateau contains some of the best preserved and most intriguing rock art found anywhere.

The specific images depicted in the rock art of the Colorado Plateau are extremely varied, but, as with all art, they fall within a culturally and environmentally determined range. This range varies from simple dots, circles, and lines to complex geometrics. Humans (both male and female), animals (bighorn sheep, deer, bison, birds, dogs, snakes, lizards, and centipedes), tools (bows and arrows, shields, flutes, atlatls, and clubs), clothing, astronomical objects (sun, moon, and stars), phenomena (rain and lightning), plants (corn and trees), supernatural entities, mythical creatures (plumed serpent), and parts of the body (handprints and footprints) are all relatively common. It should be noted that the terms used here are completely descriptive and are not meant to imply specifically what the rock art creators actually had in mind while they were producing the images. Thus, the image in a descriptive sense (i.e., "it looks like...") may be quite different from what the artisan actually had in mind at the time of manufacture. For example, what appears to us to be a bighorn sheep or snake may actually be the result of an attempt to depict a mythical clan ancestor.

Archaeologists and rock art students have long believed that the placement of rock art was extremely important to the makers. The varied locations in which known rock art appears indicate diverse functions and origins. Rock art is often located adjacent to or near habitation sites, along natural travel routes, on or adjacent to conspicuous topographic features, near water sources such as springs and tanks, and at natural camping places. However, many seemingly ideal locations, at least from our perspective, are devoid of prehistoric rock art.

Fremont style petroglyph panel, Indian Creek, Utah. Photograph by Thomas Maxwell

Newspaper Rock, Utah. Photograph by Donald E. Weaver, Jr.

The techniques used to produce rock art have been mentioned briefly in the preceding section. Now let us examine these techniques in more detail, dealing specifically with those techniques used on the Colorado Plateau.

All petroglyphs are made by removing a portion of the rock's surface in a preconceived pattern. The most common technique on the Colorado Plateau, pecking, is accomplished by either striking the rock surface with a hard, sharpened stone (direct percussion) or by hitting a chisel-like stone that is held against the rock surface with another stone, a piece of antler or bone, or a stout hunk of wood (indirect percussion). In any case, the sudden blow results in the removal of a small speck of the rock surface, usually producing a lighter colored depression or "dint." By repeating this simple operation many times, the artist could produce a recognizable image. In some cases, faint scratches of the overall design served as a guide for subsequent detailed work, but most frequently, no such guide was used.

Anyone who has experimented with these two techniques quickly learns that the use of the chisel and hammer method produces much more uniform and precise workmanship than does the hammer only method. Experiments have shown that a skilled craftsman can produce, by either method, a relatively elaborate design involving as many as five hundred to one thousand individual blows in approximately twenty minutes.

Other techniques used to produce petroglyphs or portions of petroglyphs include engraving, scratching, drilling, carving, and grinding. However, use of these techniques was relatively uncommon on the Colorado Plateau.

Pictographs usually are produced by applying paints (or less frequently, other coloring agents) to a rock surface in a preconceived arrangement. Prehistoric groups made paints by grinding naturally occurring minerals such as hematite (red), kaolin (white), and other substances like charcoal (black) into fine powder and then mixing the powder with neutral color binding agents—such as water, animal oils, and plant oils. They applied the paints in several ways, including brushes, sticks, fingers, and by blowing the paint onto the rock surface. An alternative method of applying color involves scraping a piece of mineral or charcoal on the rock surface much as we use chalk on blackboards today. This latter technique is much more common at historic sites than at prehistoric sites and is characteristic of the early historic period, especially among the Pai tribes (Yavapai, Hualapai, Paiute, etc.) and the Navajo and Apache.

Petroglyphs are found virtually all over the Colorado Plateau while pictographs apparently have a more restricted distribution. Pictographs are common in eastern Utah (especially in and north of Canyonlands National Park), the Grand Canyon, Canyon de Chelly, and the Sedona area but are uncommon or rare elsewhere. Whether this pattern is real or the biased result of uneven investigation is not known since large areas of the Colorado Plateau have never been searched systematically for rock art.

"Flute Player," Navajo National Monument
Photograph by Donald E. Weaver, Jr.

Petroglyph from Puerco Ruin area, Petrified Forest National Park. Photograph by Donald E. Weaver, Jr.

Petroglyph from area below Puerco Ruin
Photograph by Grâzina Sakalas

Crack-in-Rock, Wupatki National Monument. Photograph by Donald E. Weaver, Jr.

11

Fremont pictographs from Nine Mile Canyon, Utah. Photograph by Stephen Trimble

Sinagua petroglyphs from Horseshoe Mesa, Wupatki National Monument. Photograph by Tom Danielsen

Petroglyph from the Crack-in-Rock area of Wupatki National Monument. Photograph by Donald E. Weaver, Jr.

IMAGES ON STONE

To the casual observer, and indeed even to individuals who have carefully searched out remote sites and photographed hundreds of panels, the aesthetic appeal, coupled with the thrill of discovery, is reward enough for pursuing an interest in rock art. However, sooner or later questions always arise. What did the rock art mean? Why did the prehistoric inhabitants of the Colorado Plateau make rock art? What part did rock art play in the lives of prehistoric Native Americans? Finally, what can we learn from careful study of prehistoric rock art?

Rock art almost certainly served more than one function in prehistoric societies. In fact, the evidence strongly suggests that even within groups rock art may have played a role in a number of activities—both religious and secular. At this point, it is important to emphasize that the prehistoric inhabitants of the Colorado Plateau did not differentiate between art, religion, and everyday activities, as we do. Religion played a very important role in everyday life and was integrated into virtually every activity, as was the associated art.

Perhaps, before discussing what rock art means, it would be wise to discuss briefly some interpretations that are not supported by the evidence. One of the most persistent interpretations of rock art is that it was a form of writing—a widespread system of symbols similar to the well-known sign language of the Plains Indians. The first scientific studies of prehistoric rock art in North America were conducted in the late nineteenth century to test this very popular theory. Careful study of the evidence indicates that universal (or even widely accepted) meanings for rock act symbols were lacking. In general, scholars have discarded the writing theory, but it continues to appear in popular publications, usually championed by people who lack any training or experience in either anthropology or the methods of scientific inquiry.

Another equally unsupported interpretation concludes that rock art was merely "doodling," with no cultural significance to the makers. While some instances of rock art produced in this manner (to pass idle time or for fun) have been documented, the vast majority of prehistoric (and Native American historic) rock art does not fit this simplistic interpretation. The fact that the same designs and styles occur repeatedly in limited areas

Horseshoe Canyon, Canyonlands National Park
Photograph by Donald E. Weaver, Jr.

13

Historic rock art at Grand Wash, Arizona. Photograph by Stephen Trimble

indicates that the makers had something specific in mind. In addition, the effort and skill required to produce the rock art suggests something far more important than a mere leisurely diversion. Finally, the testimony of Native American informants, as well as numerous reported visits to rock arts sites by Native American religious leaders, strongly suggests that the rock art itself is (and was) very important.

A somewhat less common popular misinterpretation is that rock art panels, especially those dominated by abstract elements, are maps or depictions of nearby geographical features—perhaps directions to water sources or even hidden treasure. There is little hard evidence to support this theory, and only a few possible instances of rock art maps have been reported.

In a general sense, most of the prehistoric rock art of the Colorado Plateau has been interpreted by scientists as attempts to propitiate supernatural forces and to ensure individual or group prosperity. Thus, the rock art itself is directly or indirectly related to ceremo-

Horseshoe Canyon, Canyonlands National Park. Photograph by Donald E. Weaver, Jr.

Willow Springs, Arizona. Photograph by Gene Balzer

nial and religious activities. Specific functions within this general interpretation range from sympathetic hunting magic to requests for rain, from depictions of clan ancestors or mythical creatures that facilitated communication between shamans and supernatural beings to specific designs believed to foster fertility, good health, power, and success in hunting.

A concern for preserving the natural equilibrium and the well being of individuals and groups, a major function of all religions including those of Native Americans, is indicated in the prehistoric rock art of the Colorado Plateau by the relatively common occurrence of pregnancy and birth scenes of both animals and humans, the abundant use of cloud and lightning symbols, and the common depiction of animals—such as the snake and thunderbird—associated with rain and water. In the arid Southwest, rain, water, crop success, and the fertility of important game animals have been primary concerns of virtually all groups in historic times, and the same was probably true in prehistoric times as well.

Although the role of sympathetic hunting magic in the creation of prehistoric rock art has perhaps been overemphasized, hunting magic undoubtedly played a significant, if not primary, role in the production of much of the rock art of the Colorado Plateau. Hunting scenes of various types, as well as depictions of important game animals (deer, buffalo, big-

Butler Wash, Utah. Photograph by Donald E. Weaver, Jr.

Spirals, like these at Saguaro National Monument, are common in the Southwest. Photograph by Les Manevitz

Hand design from the Kaibab Plateau. Photograph by Don Keller

*Cave of Life, Petrified Forest National Park
Photograph by Stephen Trimble*

Red Tank Draw. Photograph by Gene Balzer

horn sheep), are very common, especially in areas where big game was probably abundant prehistorically. By depicting successful hunting scenes, the maker or makers attempted to ensure similar success in real life. Similarly, depictions of the animals themselves were done to guarantee an adequate supply of game. Depictions of warfare and battle, quite uncommon on the Colorado Plateau, may have had a similar function.

Much of the rock art of the Colorado Plateau is dominated by elaborate masks, humanlike figures with decorated clothing and ornate headdresses, and unusual figures (sometimes part animal and part human or ghostlike) which probably represent supernatural beings. Since masks, costumed dancers, and humanlike supernatural beings (kachinas, yeis, and other holy beings) play central roles in historic and modern Native American religious ceremonies, it is reasonable to conclude that a similar circumstance existed prehistorically. Thus, the rock art elements were probably directly related to ceremonial activities. Several scholars have suggested that many of the rock art figures were actually produced by shamans or religious leaders—or by others under their supervision. Indeed, a number of very elaborate sites are so internally homogeneous in terms of style, technique, and skill that they were probably produced by a single individual or a small group of highly trained and rigorously supervised artists.

Although it is difficult, in the case of Native American cultures (both prehistoric and historic), to separate religion from secular activities, some possible primarily nonreligious rock art functions include depictions designed to commemorate important events; to facilitate recordkeeping; to mark family, clan, or other group territorial boundaries and participation; and to mark important calendric or cyclic natural events such as the summer solstice.

The best-known example of this type of rock art is the site of Willow Springs near Tuba City. The site was a stopping place for Hopis on their way from the Hopi mesas to sacred salt deposits near the junction of the Little Colorado and Colorado rivers. As a result of repeated visits, rows of virtually identical clan

Recording at Homolovi, Arizona. Photograph by Donald E. Weav

18

symbols, representing some twenty-seven clans, have been pecked into the soft sandstone rock. Thus, the site served to commemorate one important event in an individual's life, to record a visit to the site, and to mark clan participation. In the rather unique case of Willow Springs, a sound interpretation was easily formulated since the Hopi still used the site in historic times, and a very detailed account of such a journey existed. Others possible examples of commemorative rock art are panels that appear to depict the supernova of A.D. 1054, an unusual and spectacular event unlikely to have gone unnoticed. It should be noted that even though these interpretations are primarily secular in nature the rock art undoubtedly had religious significance as well.

The interpretation of rock art is difficult, and any investigator attempting it must be willing to consider all pertinent evidence. It must be emphasized that rock art cannot be treated as a unique phenomenon distinct from the culture whose members produced it. In many cases, specific interpretation is impossible. The methods and data are simply not yet available. In such situations, it is best to accept the inevitable and hope for future insights.

Homolovi rock art. Photograph by Donald E. Weaver, Jr.

DATING ROCK ART

Determining the age of rock art is a notoriously difficult task. However, some methods do exist, and others are being developed as scientific interest in rock art increases. Indirect clues to the dating of rock art include the degree of patination or weathering, lichen growth, superimposition, subject matter, stylistic analysis, and association—both geological and cultural. Because the dating of rock art is so difficult, most researchers attempt to use all of the applicable methods in any given study.

Patina, or desert varnish, is a dark chemical coating that forms on rock surfaces, particularly in arid areas such as the Southwest. Often, petroglyphs are pecked into highly patinated surfaces. Since patina forms at a slow rate, the amount of repatination can be used as a rough measure of a petroglyph's age. Although only relative dating can be achieved at the present time, scientists working on the problem believe that studies of patination eventually will produce reliably precise absolute dates for specific petroglyphs. Relative age refers to whether a particular phenomenon or object is older or younger than another phenomenon or object, while absolute age means that the age of a particular phenomenon or object can be associated directly with a specific calendric date. In areas where patination does not occur, general rock surface weathering often provides indications of the relative ages of petroglyphs.

Lichen, a complex symbiotic plant community composed of an alga and a fungus, often grows on surfaces modified in the production of rock art. Since the rate of growth is generally quite slow, the presence and amount of lichen can be used a a relative age indicator. However, this method has been used infrequently in the Southwest because lichen growth is extremely variable and dependent on many factors.

Superimposition, one of the most widely used dating techniques, occurs when a rock art element has obviously been placed over a previously existing rock art element. On the basis of this superimposition, the two manufacturing episodes can be ordered in time. It is not possible, however, based on superimposition alone, to determine just how much time separated the two events or when either of the two events actually occurred with regard to calendar time. Many rock art sites, especially small ones, do not contain any superimposition. Thus, the method is restricted either to regional studies involving many sites or to large sites with abundant examples of superimposition.

The subject matter of rock art often provides clues to chronological placement. Rock art depicting the use of bow and arrows or firearms or showing horsemen with broad-brimmed hats must post-date the appearance of such phenomena. Thus, a petroglyph depicting the use of the bow and arrow would post-date A.D. 500. Rock art depicting either firearms or mounted horsemen must post-date A. D. 1540 and would probably be considerably later.

Photograph by Dave Edwards

Photograph by Chris Goetze

Chavez Pass area, Arizona. Photograph by Donald E. Weaver, Jr.

Stylistic analysis has been utilized in virtually every study of rock art, always in conjunction with other chronological clues, to achieve very general chronological control. The methodology involves dating rock art panels or sites to a specific time period by association, subject matter, and other factors and, then, after conducting a broad stylistic analysis, assuming that panels or sites with the same style are contemporaneous. For example, rock art sites associated with Pueblo IV locales in the Winslow area are often dominated by kachina masks. Thus, we can assume that rock art sites with kachina masks were produced in the Pueblo IV period—even if they are not associated with datable pueblos.

Petroglyphs from the Painted Desert, Arizona
Photograph by Tom Brownold

Willow Springs, Arizona. Photograph by Gene Balzer

"Newspaper Rock" is a fairly common title for panels with extensive rock art. This one is found in Petrified Forest National Park. Photograph by Dave Edwards

Association with datable geological or cultural phenomena is probably the most commonly used method of dating rock art. On the Colorado Plateau, rock art is often found in very close proximity to other archaeological sites, such as pueblos or occupied rock shelters. A relatively easy assumption to draw in such a situation is that the rock art and site are roughly contemporaneous. Since the site can usually be dated by standard archaeological techniques (tree-rings, radiocarbon, etc.), the associated rock art can also be dated. Unfortunately, there is no definite means of verifying the inferred site-rock art association in most cases.

Even more promising than the direct clues or methods discussed above are new direct-dating techniques that attempt to date the rock art manufacturing episode itself. These methods include radiocarbon and amino acid racemization dating of paints and pigments from pictographs and neutron activation analysis of patina and repatination for petroglyphs. These methods all depend on the use of sophisticated equipment and can only be done by specialists. Unfortunately, they also result in irreversible damage to the rock art elements being investigated.

Palatki Ruin, Arizona.
Photograph by Gene Balzer

Fremont pictographs from Fish Creek Cave, near Torrey, Utah. Photograph by Stephen Trimble

Detail from Newspaper Rock, Petrified Forest National Park. Photograph by Stephen Trimble

RECORDING ROCK ART

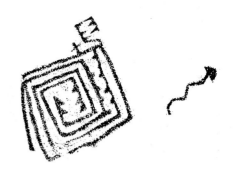

In spite of the increased scientific interest in rock art, it is still true that many of the rock art studies presently underway are being conducted by people with little or no formal training in archaeology. One of the most frequently heard questions, then, is "What is the best way to record rock art?" There is no one best way. Every site, indeed every panel, must be considered as an individual situation that may require special techniques or an unusual combination of techniques.

Archaeology, like all sciences, relies heavily on records of all types. The primary written records used for recording rock art sites are the rock art site form and the photographic log. The rock art site form is used to record all nonpictorial date about the site and to supplement the pictorial record. Universities and museums usually have a standard form specifically designed for their needs and refined over years of use. Standard data categories used include site number or name, location, size, type of rock, techniques, colors, design elements, damage, associated archaeological materials and features, natural environment, recorder, and date recorded. Space is also provided for a sketch map of the site and a map showing how to get to the site.

The photographic log is used to identify all photographs by providing basic information about each photograph taken. After all, excellent photographs of interesting rock art sites are scientifically useless unless basic information about the sites is also known.

In general, detailed photography is the most widely used method of recording rock art because it can be successfully utilized by almost anyone with access to the basic equipment (camera, light meter, film) and because it can accurately record almost every detail. Obviously, the use of color film, either slides or prints, produces a relatively accurate representation. Unfortunately, color film is notorious for its short storage life. All colors eventually fade, and the apparent advantage of color film is lost. Because of this long-term storage problem, most serious rock art scholars photograph rock art sites in both color and black-and-white.

The 35mm adjustable single lens reflex (SLR) or equivalent range-finder camera works very well for recording most rock art sites. With one set of lenses and two camera bodies, one loaded with color film and the other with black-and-white, almost anyone can produce a scientifically acceptable rock art site record. Additional lenses, flash attachments, filters, reflectors, and many other photographic accessories are useful to rock art recorders in specific situations.

The judicious use of standard photographic techniques can provide a relatively complete record of most rock art sites. However, because of poor lighting (in rock shelters for example), bad weather (rain), or very faint images, photographs are usually supplemented by tracings or scale drawings. Scale drawings are much easier to handle in the field—and producing them is less likely to damage the rock art during recording. Their

MUSEUM OF NORTHERN ARIZONA
PETROGRAPH RECORD FORM

1. SITE NO.   2. NAME
3. COUNTY   4. STATE
5. LAND STATUS   6. OWNER
7. LOCATION   8. MAP REFERENCE
9. SIZE OF PETROGRAPH AREA
10. ROCK   11. FACING
12. PETROGRAPH PANELS
13. DESIGN ELEMENTS
14. TECHNIQUE   15. STYLE
16. DINT SIZE & SPACING
17. COLORS   18. SUPERIMPOSITION
19. PATINATION   20. LICHEN
21. WEATHERING   22. VANDALISM
23. ASSOCIATED CULTURAL FEATURES
24. ASSOCIATED ARTIFACTS
25. REMARKS
26. PREVIOUS DESIGNATIONS
27. REFERENCES   28. DATE
29. RECORDER   30. PHOTOS
31. LOCATION SKETCH MAP
32. SKETCHES, TRACINGS, ETC.

quality, of course, is heavily dependent on the artistic ability of the recorder. The use of a uniform scale for an entire site expedites the process of producing scale drawings. Many recorders use colored pencils or crayons to produce faithful reproductions of pictographs. For scientific accuracy, colors should be referenced to a standard color chart. In addition to the rock art elements, it is also important to include features of the rock in the scale drawing. Smoke blackening, lichen growth, and other features could provide valuable data for interpretation. If scale drawings or tracings are not produced at the site, then some means of specifying scale must be provided for the photographic records. This is most easily done by placing a small scale in the area to be photographed. However, measurements of easily identified elements can be noted in the photographic log if you want to avoid cluttering up the photographs.

The actual site photography proceeds in logical steps from the general to the specific. After determining the general extent of the site by walking over the entire site area and the immediate vicinity, the recorder should make a series of general photographs showing terrain and vegetation. The next task is zeroing in on clusters of designs or panels. Panels are natural rock surfaces that are easily defined (i. e., one side of a single, larger boulder or a section of cliff defined by natural breaks). Panels are numbered so that they can be easily identified and mapped. Finally, the recorder obtains closeups of individual figures to illustrate unusual or especially interesting designs, manufacturing techniques, vandalism, lichen growth, and other details.

Top: Museum of Northern Arizona site form.
Middle: Panel at Picture Canyon, Arizona.
Photograph by Donald E. Weaver, Jr.
Bottom: Illustration made from the panel.
Drawing by Richard Hacker

Archaeological data brought in from the field is only fully useful if it is properly stored and available for study to qualified scholars. Thus, it is essential that the data on rock art sites be entered into a properly curated site file. Virtually all universities and museums have such files, and most will cooperate with anyone wanting to add data to the files. Anyone interested in recording rock art for scientific study would be well advised to contact a local university or museum for assistance and advice.

Left: Rock art is recorded through photographs, drawings, and site forms. Photograph by Chris Goetze
Below: Petroglyphs at Inscription Rock, a Little Colorado River site. Photograph by Gene Balzer

PROTECTING ROCK ART SITES

Rock art is an important part of our nation's cultural heritage that should be preserved for future generations. However, natural processes, including wind and water-caused erosion, rock exfoliation caused by water seepage and extreme temperatures, plant growth, and the decomposition of organic paints, all cause the deterioration and eventual loss of rock art. In fact, today only an unknown fraction of the prehistoric rock art actually produced is still evident, and at some date in the far future, all traces of that rock art will have disappeared. Even though the rock art of the Colorado Plateau is transitory, most of what is present today could last for hundreds and perhaps thousands of years. Nature usually destroys rock art at a relatively leisurely pace. Man, however, is frantically and dramatically changing the face of the earth and in the process is destroying rock art at an incredible pace. Large-scale destruction has resulted from urbanization, road and dam construction, mining activities, and other man-caused processes directly related to modern society. Individuals also contribute to the destruction by removing rock art, sometimes through the use of crowbars and dynamite, and by defacing panels with spray paint and bullets.

Of course, no concerned and well-informed citizen would knowingly damage or destroy such irreplaceable remnants of the past. To discourage the small element of our population that might purposely deface prehistoric rock art, these archaeological resources are protected by federal, state, and local laws. For example, rock art sites on federal lands are covered by the Antiquities Act of 1906 (Public Law 59-209) and the Archaeological Resources Protection Act of 1979 (Public Law 960-5). These laws apply to all lands administered by the U.S. Forest Service, the Bureau of Land Management, the National Park Service, and other federal agencies. In Arizona, federal lands comprise about seventy-one percent of the total land area. Thus, the fact that it is illegal to "...remove, damage, or otherwise alter or deface any archaeological resource (including rock paintings and rock carvings) located on public lands or Indian lands unless such activity is pursuant to a permit..." applies to most of the rock art in Arizona. Similar circumstances are true for Colorado, Utah, and New Mexico. Penalties include fines up to $20,000 and up to two years in prison for the first offense and fines up to $100,000 and up to five years in prison for the second offense.

The rock art sites described in the following lists are primarily those that are readily accessible by road or in an area administered for public recreation and are at least partially protected by some form of federal or state agency on-site supervision. The lists are not complete by any means but should serve as a general introduction to Colorado Plateau rock art. Anyone really interested in recording rock art must be willing and able to seek out remote nooks and crannies. Many of the most impressive and interesting rock art sites can only be reached by walking for miles, and in some cases days, over rough terrain. Once started on the quest, however, the only limits are imposed by physical stamina and the breadth of our imagination.

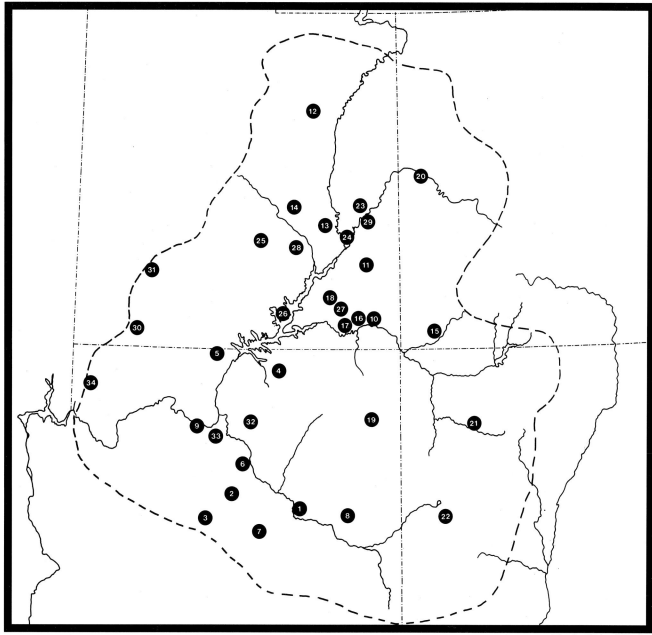

Map by Richard Hacker

ROCK ART SITE LOCATIONS

1. Homolovi
2. Picture Canyon
3. Palatki and Honanki
4. Navajo National Monument
5. Paria Canyon
6. Wupatki National Monument
7. Chavez Pass
8. Petrified Forest National Park
9. Grand Canyon National Park
10. Sand Island
11. Newspaper Rock State
   Historical Monument
12. Nine Mile Canyon

13. Horseshoe Canyon, Canyonlands
   National Park
14. Temple Mountain Wash
15. Mesa Verde National Park
16. Butler Wash
17. River House Ruin
18. Natural Bridges National Monument
19. Canyon De Chelly
   National Monument
20. Colorado National Monument
21. Chaco Canyon National Monument
22. El Morro National Monument
23. Arches National Park

24. Canyonlands National Park
25. Capitol Reef National Park
26. Glen Canyon National Recreation Area
27. Grand Gulch
28. Hog Springs
29. Utah 279 Sites
30. Zion National Park
31. Parawon Gap
32. Willow Springs
33. Kaibab Plateau
34. Grand Wash

SOUTHWESTERN ROCK ART SITES

Arizona

Canyon de Chelly National Monument
Rock art sites, like all archaeological sites in the monument, except White House, can only be visited with organized Park Service tours or an authorized Navajo guide. Inquire at the monument visitor center.

Homolovi II
Homolovi II, located on Arizona state land on the north side of the Little Colorado River west of Winslow, has many associated petroglyphs. A caretaker in residence at Homolovi I, 3 miles east of Homolovi II, monitors visitors.

Navajo National Monument
All of the large cliff dwellings have associated rock art. Betatakin is the most easily visited during regularly scheduled ranger-guided hiking tours. Both pictographs and petroglyphs occur. Inquire at the monument center.

Paria Canyon Primitive Area
Numerous petroglyphs occur in Paria Canyon. The most impressive panels are located in the middle and lower reaches of the canyon and are accessible only by backpacking. Prior registration with the Bureau of Land Management is required.

Palatki and Honanki
Both sites, within the Coconino National Forest southwest of Sedona, are large cliff dwellings with many associated pictographs. Honanki has been badly vandalized because of its accessibility. Palatki can only be visited with special permission. Contact Forest Rangers.

Petrified Forest National Park
Abundant rock art can be viewed easily at the Park, Puerco Ruin, and Newspaper Rock. Other remote rock art locales require special permission. Inquire at the park visitor center.

Wupatki National Monument
Petroglyphs can be found near most of the major sites. The largest concentration, around Crack-in-Rock, can be visited only with special permission. Inquire at the monument visitor center.

Colorado

Colorado National Monument
One site in No Thoroughfare Canyon is accessible by hiking. Other sites in the monument can be visited with special permission obtained at monument headquarters.

Mesa Verde National Park
A few petroglyphs are associated with the major sites in the park. Pictograph Point, the largest rock art site in the park can be visited by hiking a 2.3 mile trail round trip. Register at park headquarters. One large petroglyph panel and several small nearby panels can be viewed.

New Mexico

Chaco Canyon National Monument
Many petroglyphs and a few pictographs are associated with the large sites in Chaco Canyon. Some can be seen from the established trails. Off trail visits require special permission.

El Morro National Monument
Although most of the rock inscriptions in this monument are historic, prehistoric petroglyphs can also be viewed along the established trails.

Utah

Arches National Park
Several small rock art sites are within the park. They can be reached by short walks. Inquire at the park visitor center.

Canyonlands National Park
Numerous pictograph and petroglyphs have been recorded in the park. Major sites occur in Salt Creek, Horseshoe, and Range Canyons. Most are accessible only with four wheel drive vehicles, by hiking or backpacking, or by boat.

Capitol Reef National Park
Numerous rock art sites have been found in the park. Most are located along the Fremont River, and many are accessible only with four wheel drive vehicles or by hiking. Some sites can be viewed easily on short walks from Hwy 24. Inquire at the park visitor center.

Glen Canyon National Recreation Area
Although many rock art sites have been covered by the lake, others are still accessible by boat, hiking, and four wheel drive vehicles. Some locations are listed in commercially available guide books and maps.

Grand Gulch Primitive Area
Numerous rock art sites, often associated with structures, can be seen within Grand Gulch and its side canyons northwest of Mexican Hat. Accessible only by backpacking. Prior registration with the Bureau of Land Management is required.

Hog Springs
An easily visited rock shelter with pictographs is located near this roadside picnic area 37 mi south of Hanksville on Utah Hwy 95.

Natural Bridges National Monument
Both petroglyphs and pictographs can be viewed at or near Sipapu, Kachina, and Owachoma bridges. Accessible only by hiking steep trails. Inquire at the monument visitor center.

Newpaper Rock State Historical Monument
Northwest of Monticello off Hwy 163 and 12 miles in on the road to Canyonlands National Park, a large cliff covered with petroglyphs and protected by a chainlink fence can be visited. Smaller sites are located downstream along Indian Creek.

Nine Mile Canyon
Northwest of Price off Hwy 6 about 20 miles on the road to Myton. Numerous petroglyphs and pictographs occur on the cliffs along Nine Mile Creek.

Temple Mountain Wash
North of Hanksville off Hwy 24 just past the Goblin Valley State Park Turnoff, a single large pictograph panel is located high under an overhang on the north side of the road where the canyon narrows. Binoculars and a telephoto lens would be useful.

Sand Island
A large petroglyph site, protected by a chainlink fence, is located downriver ½ mi from the Sand Island campground road 3 miles west of Bluff off Hwy 163.

Zion National Park
Several small pictograph and petroglyph sites can be visited within the park. All are accessible by short walks. Inquire at the park visitor center.

Nine Mile Canyon, Utah. Photograph by Donald E. Weaver, Jr.

River House ruin on the San Juan River. Photograph by Christa J. Sadler

SUGGESTED READINGS

Barnes, F. A.
1982 *Canyon Country Prehistoric Rock Art.* Wasatch Publishers, Salt Lake City

Written for the general public as a tourist guide, this book contains many inaccuracies and erroneous conclusions. However, it is profusely illustrated and is the most complete general introduction to the prehistoric rock art of the Colorado Plateau. Paperback.

Castleton, Kenneth B., M.D.
1978 *Petroglyphs and Pictographs of Utah. Vol. I & II.* Utah Museum of Natural History, Salt Lake City.

Following a very brief summary, numerous sites scattered throughout Utah are described and illustrated. Profusely illustrated with photographs, drawings and maps.

Grant, Campbell
1967 *Rock Art of the American Indian.* Thomas Y. Crowell, New York.

The best general introduction to rock art, this book covers only the United States and Canada. Profusely illustrated. Available in paperback.

1980 *Indian Rock Art of the Southwest.* School of American Research Southwest Indian Art Series, School of American Research, Santa Fe.

A good general summary by an acknowledged expert in the field of rock art, this book concentrates on New Mexico and Utah but also includes sections of Arizona and Colorado. Profusely illustrated including maps.

Turner, Christy G., III
1963 *Petrographs of the Glen Canyon Region.* Museum of Northern Arizona Bulletin, No. 38, Flagstaff.

A pioneering study of rock art on the Colorado Plateau, this report documents the rock art destroyed by the construction of Glen Canyon Dam and the filling of Lake Powell. Some of the sites can still be visited by boat. Well illustrated.

ABOUT THE AUTHOR

Donald E. Weaver, Jr. received his Doctor of Philosophy degree in anthropology from Arizona State University in 1978. Former Chief Archaeologist at the Museum of Northern Arizona, he currently is working on a monograph dealing with the petroglyphs of the Winslow area as well as papers on central Arizona pictographs and Sinaguan rock art.

Plateau Managing Editor: Diana Clark Lubick
Editorial Assistant: D.A. Boyd
Graphic Design by Libby Jennings
Typography by MacTypeNet
Color Separations by Color Masters
Printing by Land O'Sun Printers

Rock art motifs by Richard Hacker